CLASSIFIED

SECRETS YOU'RE NOT SUPPOSED TO KNOW

PRIVACY IN THE DIGITAL WORLD

Who's Watching Us?

Ellis Roxburgh

LUCENT PRESS

Published in 2019 by
Lucent Press, an Imprint of Greenhaven Publishing, LLC
353 3rd Avenue
Suite 255
New York, NY 10010

For Brown Bear Books Ltd:
Managing Editor: Tim Cooke
Designer: Lynne Lennon
Children's Publisher: Anne O'Daly
Design Manager: Keith Davis
Editorial Director: Lindsey Lowe
Picture Manager: Sophie Mortimer

Picture Credits
t=top, c=center, b=bottom, l=left, r=right
Interior: Alamy: Stacy Walsh/Rosenstock, 15; Dreamstime: Andrey Popv, 12, Ginger Saunders, 26, Zhukovsky, 11r; istockphoto: Willem Jaap, 7; LAPD: 11t; Public Domain: Matt Britt/The Opte Project, 40, Bundesrepublik Deutschland, 28, National Security Agency, 24, NoCultureIcons/Digitale Gesellschaft, 25, United States Capitol, 39; Shutterstock: aphotostory, 34, Franck Boston, 13, Alexandru Chiriac, 37, Ivan Cholakov, 1, Crepics VOF, 43, George Dukin, 18, Evan El-Amin, 44, Everett Historical, 42, Aleksandra Gigowsa, 20, GPointStudio, 17, A Katz, 21, George JMC Little, 19, Jacob Lund, 16, Dmitri Maar, 27, Benny Marty, 45, Monkey Business Images, 5, REDPIXEL.PL, 31, Joseph Sohm, 33, testing, 4, Tongcorn Photography, 35, Tupungato, 8, Vlicha, 23; Thinkstock: Dragon Images, 32, istockphoto, 9, Ryan McVay, 36; Topfoto: The Image Works, 29. US Government: FBI, 10.
Front cover: Ivan Cholakov/Shutterstock

Cataloging-in-Publication Data

Names: Roxburgh, Ellis.
Title: Privacy in the digital world: who's watching us? / Ellis Roxburgh.
Description: New York : Lucent Press, 2019. | Series: Classified: secrets you're not supposed to know | Includes glossary and index.
Identifiers: ISBN 9781534564411 (pbk.) | ISBN 9781534564398 (library bound) | ISBN 9781534564404 (ebook)
Subjects: LCSH: Internet and teenagers--Juvenile literature. | Privacy, Right of--Juvenile literature. | Computer security--Juvenile literature. | Internet--Moral and ethical aspects--Juvenile literature.
Classification: LCC HQ799.2.I5 R69 2019 | DDC 004.67'80835--dc23
Manufactured in the United States of America

CPSIA Compliance Information: Batch #BS18KL
For further information contact Rosen Publishing, New York, New York at 1-800-237-9932

CONTENTS

PRIVACY UNDER PRESSURE

Modern technology has revolutionized daily life. This has brought great benefits, but some people fear it also threatens traditional values, such as privacy.

Today, almost everyone has a cell phone and a tablet or computer. Millions of people interact with their friends on social media. Shoppers can buy everything they need with a credit card and the Internet. But these same devices that have made many aspects of life easier also leave their users vulnerable to an increased risk of having their behavior monitored by governments, businesses, or even criminals.

>> **Cell Phones in Beijing**
Information is stored about millions of individual communications anywhere in the world.

>> **Credit Card Trail** Using a credit card allows retailers to build up a record of a person's buying habits.

KEEPING A BALANCE

Governments use the information they collect about the behavior of large numbers of people to help plan more effectively for the needs of their citizens. Law enforcement agencies monitor communications to detect crimes or acts of terrorism that are being planned. Retailers use information about buying habits to target advertising and special offers. But these benefits come at the cost of making individuals' private communications accessible to others. Some people think the sacrifice is a price worth paying. Others fear that it opens the way for more interference in our daily lives.

YOU ARE BEING WATCHED

Almost anywhere you go, someone knows what you're doing. Security cameras watch streets, shopping malls, airports, apartment blocks, and even schools.

There has been a huge growth in the number of video cameras in the streets in the last 20 years, but the first **closed-circuit TV** (CCTV) in the United States was installed in 1968 by police in Olean, New York, to prevent street crime.

ON CAMERA

Video **surveillance** is now common in cities. In 2015, Beijing in China had around 470,000 cameras; London in Great Britain had 420,000. There are fewer cameras in US cities than in other countries, but the New York Police Department (NYPD) has more than 9,000 CCTV cameras. It uses them to watch for suspicious activity, as well as to monitor traffic.

>> Offering Protection
Surveillance cameras are meant to make deserted parts of the city safer.

FAST FACTS

ON CAMERA

There are around 30 million surveillance cameras in the United States. The United Kingdom has an estimated 1.85 million CCTV cameras. That is one camera for every 30 people. On an average day, a British citizen is picked up on more than 70 separate cameras.

Some people say that these cameras increase personal security for everyone. However, critics argue that they are an invasion of privacy. These critics believe that citizens should be entitled to be able to move around without having their movements traced. In a free society, they say, no one should have the power to record a citizen's lawful actions.

BEHIND THE CAMERA

Surveillance can be carried out by a range of organizations and individuals, and for many purposes. Many cameras belong to branches of government, such as law enforcement, intelligence agencies, and transit authorities.

>> Traffic Camera
Cameras are used at major intersections to monitor traffic flow.

WHAT DO YOU THINK?

Many people see the use of CCTV as an invasion of privacy. Its supporters argue that cameras are normally used in places that are already public. They say that people cannot claim a right to privacy if they are in a public place. Critics argue that it is not the filming itself that is the problem. They object to the act of tracking someone or recording their movements. What do you think? Does being on camera invade your privacy?

Other CCTV cameras are run by private security firms that guard places such as shopping malls. The owners of stores often install cameras to watch for thieves. Landlords or building boards may place cameras in their properties to check for intruders. Some families even have cameras in their homes to deter burglars.

MORE USES

Cameras have other uses, too. Drivers and cyclists sometimes use dashboard cameras or head cameras to record their journeys in case of accidents or other unexpected events.

04-15-2013 14:37:40

FOR AND AGAINST

In 2013, CCTV captured the explosion of a terrorist bomb near the end of the Boston Marathon. Three people died, and hundreds were injured. Police used CCTV images (right) to identify the suspects as two brothers. Within four days, one of the brothers had been killed and the other captured. However, the cameras had not stopped the brothers planting the bomb or enabled security personnel to find and disable it. Is this case an argument for or against surveillance cameras?

CAMERAS AND CRIME

Supporters of CCTV argue that it helps to prevent crime. Law enforcement agencies, for example, say that cameras may help detect activity that might lead to the discovery of a terrorist plot. Cameras also alert police to potential **antisocial** behavior, such as when gang members gather in a particular place. Crime has fallen in places where cameras have been installed, such as in parking lots.

>> **Thieves on Camera** Store footage shows a robbery taking place.

However, people who want fewer cameras argue that there is little **statistical** evidence that surveillance prevents crime. They say that CCTV footage helps catch criminals after a crime, rather than helping to stop the crime.

>> **NYPD Camera** Supporters of CCTV argue that just the presence of a camera helps deter criminals.

> **>> Apartment Block**
> Many security guards have no official authority. Should they be allowed to monitor the behavior of private individuals?

TRACKING INDIVIDUALS

Civil liberties groups oppose CCTV because they are concerned about the state's ability to track its citizens. Since 2011, the NYPD has used facial-recognition software to scan CCTV footage in case it recognizes a known criminal. In 2017, the city announced the creation of a transportation monitoring system that would photograph license plates and driver faces at key points such as bridges. Opponents of CCTV surveillance argue that this might allow the city to build up a picture of an individual's movements, which is illegal.

DELICATE BALANCE

Some citizens also object to being watched by cameras. In apartment blocks, for example, many residents do not wish to be photographed as they come and go at different times, or to have their visitors monitored. They may have perfectly legitimate private reasons for their activities. However, building managers report that most residents are willing to allow cameras in public areas such as elevators, corridors, and lobbies as long as they believe the cameras will improve security. The equation is common to all debates about surveillance: striking the balance between intrusion and security.

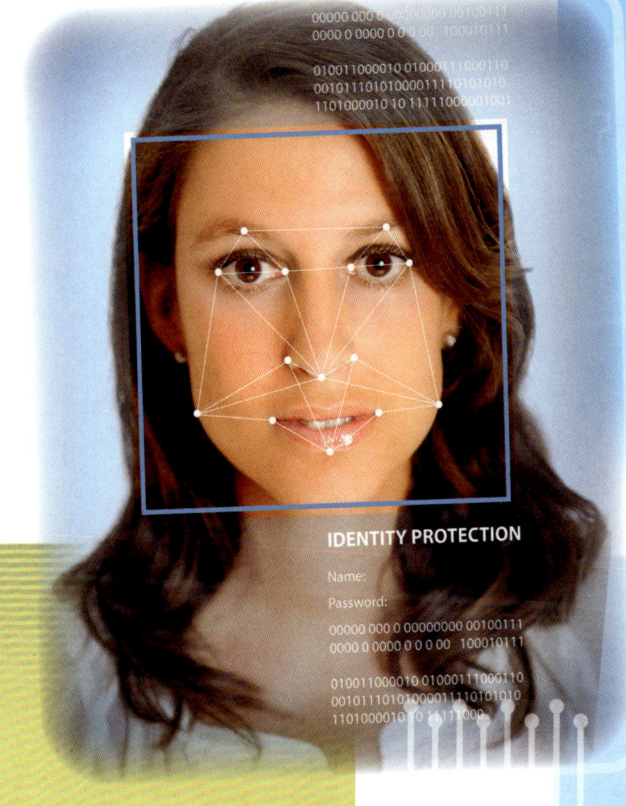

IDENTITY PROTECTION

Name:

Password:

UNIQUE ID

Facial recognition software uses unique dimensions of an individual's features to compare a CCTV image to a central database of images. The software uses algorithms to analyze the relative size of features such as eyes, ears, nose, and lips. It compares a photograph against a database of faces to find a match.

TOP SECRET

SOURCES OF INFORMATION

People's everyday activities often reveal information about themselves. Sometimes people are not even aware that this information is being gathered.

The information can be used by criminals to plan crimes. It can be used by retailers to target consumers. Or it might be used by governments to monitor the actions of citizens, both in general terms and by targeting specific individuals. The growth of the Internet and of mobile technology such as cell phones has greatly increased the number of ways in which people reveal private information. However, information can be gathered from a wide range of sources, such as credit cards, **loyalty programs**, or even library books.

PATRIOT ACT

The U.S. government began the large-scale collection of information about its citizens after the terrorist actions of 9/11 in 2001. The al-Qaeda group used airplanes to attack targets in New York City, Pennsylvania, and Washington, D.C.

>> **Twin Towers**
The World Trade Center in New York City was destroyed by terrorist attacks in 2001.

FAST FACTS

TERRORIST ALERT

Law enforcement agencies began to pay serious attention to monitoring cell phones and Internet activity after the growth of terrorism in the late 1900s. Terrorists used emails and mobile phones to plan attacks such as those of 9/11 in 2001.

In response to the attack, the government introduced the USA PATRIOT Act. The act gave law enforcement and intelligence agencies the power to access people's business records, medical records, and educational records. It made it easier for federal agencies to monitor the phones, emails, and behavior of suspected terrorists. The act even gave the agencies the right to access people's library records to find out what books they had borrowed. The agencies wanted to know if people were reading about Islamist politics, for example, or how to make a bomb or fly an airplane. While the government argued that such records might flag signs of a terror plot, critics argued that this was an unjustifiable invasion of privacy. Many of the act's provisions lapsed after 10 years, in 2011.

>> **Library Shelves** The Patriot Act gave governments the right to find out what books people borrowed from public libraries.

WHAT DO YOU THINK?

In 2017, the app Snapchat introduced Snap Map, a feature that allowed users to track the location of their friends. It was intended to allow people to find each other in crowded locations. However, many parents were alarmed that the highly accurate maps might allow bullies to track their victims. The maps might also lead to social exclusion, such as by showing someone that they were excluded from an event all their friends attended. Do you think people were right to be concerned?

>> **Music Festival**
Snap Map helps you locate your friends in crowded places.

ELECTRONIC COMMUNICATIONS

One common way in which people give away information about themselves is by using cell phones and tablets. These electronic devices often include **location services**. The services are intended to make sure that users have access to information that relates to wherever they are, such as the location of restaurants or weather forecasts. But the same services also track the position of the devices. This enables phone companies to map users' movements. Potentially, this information is also available to anyone who can hack into it. For example, criminals could learn when a home is empty so they can plan a **burglary**.

Even if location services are switched off, cell phones still reveal information about the user's location. Cell phones use signals from communications masts. Every time someone makes a call or sends a text message, the phone company collects data from the masts that relay the signals. That makes it relatively easy to track the movements of the device user. Although this information is kept by the phone companies, it can be made available to law-enforcement agencies.

Phone companies argue that their data is **"anonymized."** They say it is impossible to distinguish individual details from the massive amounts of information. Critics argue that it is relatively easy to access individual data.

>> **Communications Mast**
Masts record information about all phones used in their area, or cell.

FOR AND AGAINST

Online retailers record what customers browse and buy. They say this allows them to target promotions, which benefits the customer. Critics say that the retailers do not simply use the information themselves but also sell it to other organizations. Political parties, for example, sometimes use shopping habits to guess a person's likely party loyalties and to target individuals accordingly.

>> Online Shopping
Does making a purchase make you a target for unwanted messages?

ONLINE DATA

Electronic communications reveal more information about users than they realize. Posted photographs of people at home might identify an address, while greetings from friends reveal someone's date of birth. These two pieces of information can form the basis of identity theft. There have also been reports of criminals identifying items to steal after seeing them on social media. However, social media can also work to solve crimes. Police forces have made arrests and recovered stolen goods when criminals post details of their crimes online.

SHOPPING SERVICES

Information is collected by many commercial firms without individuals' knowledge or agreement. Retailers have developed sophisticated ways to analyze the buying habits of shoppers through loyalty cards and credit cards. Loyalty programs that reward shoppers for repeat purchases have existed for centuries.

In the late 1900s, U.S. airlines such as American Airlines and United introduced loyalty cards for frequent flyers. They were soon followed by many other retailers with their own loyalty cards. Like earlier loyalty programs, the cards give shoppers access to discounts. Because the card is scanned each time it is used, however, it also allows stores to track an individual's shopping patterns more closely. Data analysts use software to mine the data then target groups of consumers with offers tailored to them. Some purchasers are happy to surrender some privacy for the **convenience** of receiving discounts on items they might actually want. Others are wary of revealing this kind of information.

>> **Loyalty Card** Every time a customer uses a loyalty card or club card, a retailer can track his or her purchases.

WORRYING ACCURACY

This type of analysis can be highly accurate. Women often make subtle changes in what they buy when they become pregnant. They might switch to unscented soaps, for example. In 2012, a story was reported of a father in the United States complaining to the retailer Target. He was angry that the retailer had sent his teenage daughter coupons for baby products. Target's computer analysis of her shopping habits meant that she was included in a mail-out for newly pregnant women. The father withdrew his complaint after his daughter admitted that she was pregnant. Target's algorithms had figured this out before she told her family.

>> **Giant Retailer** Retailers now habitually record what people buy in order to figure out what they are likely to buy in the future.

GATHERING INFORMATION

Many organizations are eager to learn about individuals for many different purposes.

Governments collect data about their citizens and about visitors to their countries. The Social Security Administration issues numbers to every citizen and keeps records of their address, marital status, number of children, and so on. The Internal Revenue Service keeps records of employment and income. School boards have records of students' attendance, behavior, and academic achievements. Police departments keep criminal records, and may store fingerprints or **DNA** samples. U.S. Customs and Border Protection records the passports of people entering the country.

Many people argue that governments need this information. Without accurate data, they say, it would be impossible for governments to plan spending, for states to anticipate the demand for school places, or for hospitals to be sure to have adequate supplies of drugs. These people think governments should have information about people for practical reasons.

YOU'RE ON FILE

In most countries, records about individuals are kept from birth. It is a legal requirement that all births are registered by physicians or parents. There are numerous other occasions when people are required to file information with officials, such as when children reach school age, when people require a social security number, and when someone dies.

>> **Fingerprints** Police forces take and store fingerprints and DNA evidence from criminals.

>> **NSA Headquarters** The NSA has so many computers, it is the largest consumer of electricity in Maryland.

TRUST IN THE GOVERNMENT?

Not everyone accepts this argument. Since the creation of the United States after the American Revolution, many Americans have been suspicious of government agencies, particularly federal agencies. They instinctively oppose what they condemn as "big government." They believe the state interferes too much in the lives of individual citizens.

This belief was reinforced in 2013. Edward Snowden, a contractor working for the National Security Agency (NSA), leaked millions of classified documents. The documents showed that the NSA habitually monitored people's emails and phone calls. This activity was illegal, but the NSA argued that it was necessary to prevent terrorist activity. There was great controversy about the scale of this secret invasion of privacy. The NSA had even **eavesdropped** on the telephone conversations of the German chancellor, Angela Merkel.

WHAT DO YOU THINK?

The U.S. contractor Edward Snowden leaked millions of classified documents in 2013. They showed that the U.S. government has been illegally monitoring communications. Snowden fled to Russia to avoid punishment. He has been condemned as a traitor against his country but also hailed as a hero for revealing the government's actions. What do you think?

>> **Privacy Protest** People against U.S. monitoring of German citizens' communications protest in Berlin in 2013.

GOING OFF GRID

Some people avoid surveillance by living "off grid." Their homes are not linked to the power grid or served by the U.S. Mail. They do not use bank accounts or credit cards, preferring to rely on cash payments or **barter**. They do not enroll their children in formal education. If someone gets sick, they are treated with traditional folk remedies by a skilled local practitioner. In 2013, it was estimated that 180,000 American families were living off grid—and around 1.7 billion people were doing so around the world.

QUESTIONS OF IDENTITY

Even many people who do not live off grid remain distrustful of government invasions of privacy. One example is identity (ID) cards. Some form of identity document or electronic record of a person's identity is required in many countries. In some of those countries, such as Belgium, Spain, and Colombia, citizens must carry their ID at all times.

In others, such as Germany, ID is required but does not have to be carried. In South America, Argentina, Brazil, and Chile have ID cards. In Asia, China, Indonesia, and South Korea are among the countries with required ID cards.

Identity cards are controversial. In 2006, the British government passed an act that required all British citizens to carry identity cards. ID information would be stored in a national **database**. Supporters of the cards said this would help prevent crime and acts of terrorism. After a public campaign about the invasion of privacy, the act was repealed in 2011.

>> **Street View Car** Google cars photograph anyone on the street as they pass, as well as the street itself.

FOR AND AGAINST

Google Street View plans to record images of the whole planet to create an online photographic atlas. It uses cars equipped with cameras (right) to take photographs of every city, town, and village. Critics argue that because these photographs show identifiable individuals or glimpses into homes through open windows, they are invasions of privacy. Google claims it only photographs what is on public display, and so cannot breach privacy.

DIGITAL IDENTITY

Since 2009, the Indian government has been gathering **biometric** data, such as fingerprints and iris scans, on nearly a billion citizens. The data is stored in a high-security system. Citizens had to register to receive a unique 12-digit identity number, which allows them to access all government services. In 2017 the Indian High Court ruled that the program was illegal because it broke the country's laws on individual privacy. The program remained operational, but citizens no longer had to have an identity number to access services.

The United States does not have a national identity card. However, there are times when people have to show identification, such as a driver's license when driving a vehicle. In some states, law enforcement officers can ask someone for ID if they think he or she is acting suspiciously.

FOR AND AGAINST

Some people think having to carry a card to prove their identity is reasonable in order to prevent terrorism, identity theft, or illegal immigration. Other people think such cards have no place in a democracy. They associate such cards with police states where no one has the freedom to move around without being challenged.

>> **Border Patrol** An officer checks the identity of a suspected illegal immigrant to the United States.

Identification is also needed for certain transactions, such as purchasing tobacco or alcohol. Noncitizens in the United States can be asked to produce a visa or a passport. Immigrants may also be asked to prove their resident status. Such challenges usually affect members of poorer Hispanic communities, who are most likely to be suspected of being illegal immigrants. Critics of the system warn that the United States is becoming a society in which the poor and underprivileged are under greater pressure to prove their identity than the rich.

SPIES IN YOUR COMPUTER

Every time people go online, it is possible that their actions are being watched. Crimimals have figured out ways to monitor computer activity via the Internet.

Hackers use various ways to gain private information from people's computers. One of the most effective ways is to **hack** into the electronic records of large corporations, banks, or retailers. This allows hackers to steal the names, addresses, Internet search histories, and credit card transactions for potentially millions of accounts in a single attack. The hackers then sell the information to other criminals, who use the details to steal money from the victims' bank accounts. Hackers also target individual users by using software that tracks the websites the individuals visit, the information they key in, and the personal data and passwords stored on the computer.

>> **Hacking** Firms are involved in a constant battle to keep electronic data safe from hackers.

```
ant;}
ortant; height: 73px !important
!important; height: 225px; padding: 5px 0px !important
px !important;}
ght: 25px !important;}
x !important;}
lect: none; -khtml-user-select: none; -moz-user-select:
ointer;transform: rotate(180deg);transition: all 0.5s e
: 280px;}
x;}
none !important;}
!important;}
gin-bottom: 5px
nt-size: 10px; m
10px;}
ft: 3px; border-
10px;}
#fff !important;
{border-top-colo
shadow: 0 1px 4px rgba(0,0,0,.2); box-shadow: 0 1px 4px
!important;}
2px 0px !important; }
```

FAST FACTS

CYBERCRIME

The Internet has changed the world in the last few decades. It has also changed the nature of crime. Cyber criminals steal information from individuals and companies by hacking into their accounts. Security experts work constantly to figure out more sophisticated ways to encrypt and protect information. One of the most effective ways they work is by persuading former hackers to cooperate with them to figure out how to prevent future hacking.

PRIVATE VS. PUBLIC

People in the comfort of their homes often feel as if the Internet and social media are intimate, private methods of communication. Experts warn that they are the opposite. Almost anyone who uses computers for communication has made errors or revealed information that might embarrass them if it became public. People may have been rude about their workmates, for example, or looked at politically extreme videos. People may have posted photographs or said things on social media that they might later regret, especially if they were widely circulated.

>> **Personal Computer**
Virtually nothing we do via the Internet is as secure as it feels to us.

FOR AND AGAINST

Some web-based apps allow people to control their homes remotely. People can switch on or off their heating, for example, or see who is at their door. However, while this can be convenient, remote signals are always vulnerable to hacking. Such apps might leave homeowners open to attack by malicious or mischievous hackers or criminals.

People have had to leave their jobs because of photographs they have posted online. Politicians have had to resign because of statements they made on social media, in some cases before they were even elected.

VULNERABLE INFORMATION

Data about web searches and site visits are recorded in a computer's **cache**. This is a temporary folder that can be deleted, although it is difficult to erase all details of a search history. In addition, search histories are recorded by Internet Service Providers (**ISPs**), where a user cannot erase them.

Security experts say this information could be accessed not only by criminals, but also by hostile governments or organizations that might be prepared to pay to obtain it.

The stored information in a cache is often used to target individuals for retail promotions. But there is also potential for crimes such as blackmail and identity theft. Criminals could threaten to reveal details of Internet use or email communication unless they are paid. Or they could use people's identities to make purchases or steal money from bank accounts.

CHINA'S FIREWALL

The communist government in China limits its citizens' access to the Internet. In 2017, it announced a program by which people would only be able to post online or on social media having registered their real name and proved their identity, thus limiting the ability of people to post anonymous criticism of the government.

>> Great Wall of China
The government limits the Internet in China with what is called the Great Firewall of China.

PHISHING AND VIRUSES

In Internet "phishing," criminals send emails containing links to what appear to be genuine websites for banks or other organizations. They ask users to input sensitive account information, which the criminals then use to steal from the genuine accounts. According to one estimate, $5 billion was stolen around the world in 2014 using phishing techniques.

Another form of Internet crime uses a virus to infect a computer. A keylogger virus records every keystroke made by a user. It identifies strings of figures that might be a bank account and looks for related passwords. Criminals use the information to take money from bank accounts. In 2016, criminals may have used viruses to gather the information to launch a massive cyber attack on Tesco Bank in the United Kingdom. The thieves raided the accounts of 9,000 customers, stealing a total of £2.5 million, or about $3 million.

DATA BREACHES

Some experts believe that the criminals behind the raid had collected data from individual customers using phishing or viruses. Others argue that they may have found a weakness in the bank's security systems. Still others say that the most likely explanation is a disgruntled employee at the bank selling customers' details to the criminals. Unauthorized releases of information are **data breaches**. They have grown in number and in size in the last two decades. In 2014, there were 783 recorded data breaches in the United States, and more than 85 million records were exposed.

>> **Internet Café** Accessing your accounts remotely is convenient but shared computers are potentially more vulnerable than private ones.

A large data breach affected a company called Court Ventures, which was bought by US credit reporting agency Experian in 2012. Before Experian bought the company, criminals in Vietnam used Court Ventures to access the records of up to 200 million people. They sold credit card and social security numbers to other criminals.

>> **Servers** Cloud data is shared among a network of millions of servers around the world.

WHAT DO YOU THINK?

Since 2006, people are increasingly storing files and applications on "cloud" devices. These are centralized servers that hold enormous amounts of information. These servers are more secure than individual computers, but the very fact that they are linked to the Internet means that they could be vulnerable to attack. Because they store so much data, they are also likely to attract more attention from hackers than personal computers. Would you be happier to store your data in the Cloud or on your own devices?

PRIVACY AND THE LAW

The growth of the Internet, **data mining,** and cell phone use has brought great challenges to traditional legal definitions of privacy.

Privacy is widely seen as a fundamental human right. It has long been accepted that people should be able to expect their own homes to be private spaces and to make decisions about their beliefs and behavior according to their own conscience, as long as their actions are within the law.

CHANGING DEFINITIONS

In most countries, people also have the right to expect that details about their lives—such as how much they earn, their tax returns, or their medical history—are not made public. However, with the rise of the Internet, some legal experts believe that traditional ideas about privacy are under threat. In particular, they are concerned about whether it is possible to keep individuals' personal details private in a digital age. Some observers go further, asserting that "Privacy is dead."

FAST FACTS

LONG DEBATE

The debate about digital privacy is the latest stage in a debate that is centuries old. When the Founders of the United States wrote the world's first national constitution in 1787 they debated the rights of the citizen to be left alone to live their own lives against the right of the government to monitor their actions.

>> **Founders**
The Founders of the United States did not see the need to grant Americans a specific right of privacy.

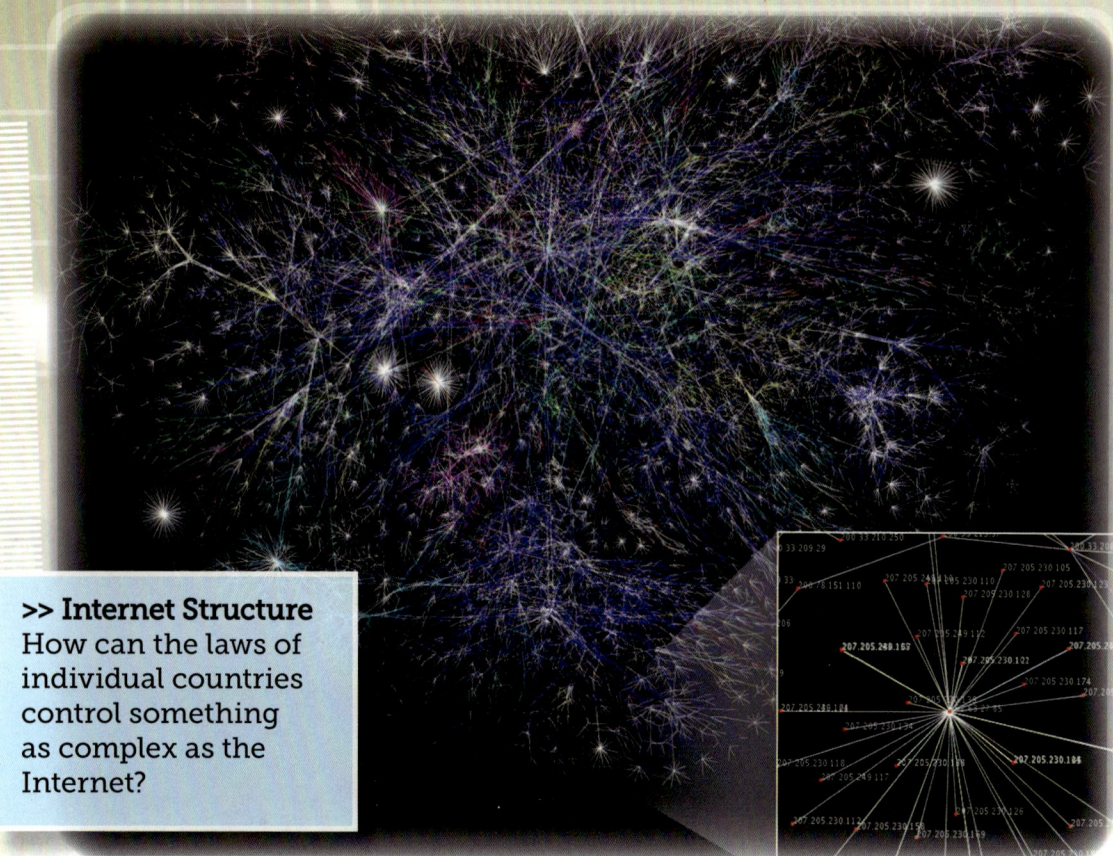

>> **Internet Structure**
How can the laws of individual countries control something as complex as the Internet?

LEAVING TRACES

The greatest potential danger to privacy, according to experts, is that the Internet, social media, and other digital devices leave evidence of users' behavior that can become widely accessible. This information might be made public because of criminal activity such as phishing, because of an accidental release of data by an organization, or because of carelessness by users. This would be a breach of privacy in itself—but it might also leave users vulnerable to **blackmailers** or identity thieves. It might also enable the committing of fraud, such as illegal voter registration and voting.

LAWS AND THE WEB

Around the world, countries have attempted to update their privacy laws to deal with rapidly changing technology. Different countries have drafted different laws, but no one has yet been able fully to solve the problem. In addition, the Internet is by its nature difficult to make subject to laws. While laws apply in particular **jurisdictions**, the Internet does not operate within national boundaries. What laws should apply to a website? Those of the country where the website was created, or of the country where it is stored on servers, or in the country of the person using it?

FOR AND AGAINST

Anonymous is a group of computer hackers who are known for wearing Guy Fawkes masks when they appear in public. Anonymous launches cyber attacks against businesses and governments. It claims to act in the public interest and against attempts to control the Internet. Its critics say that the group are little more than **anarchists** and criminals.

>> **Bill of Rights** The U.S. Constitution and its amendments do not explicitly guarantee a right to privacy.

THE EUROPEAN UNION

In 2016, the European Union introduced the General Data Protection Regulation (GDPR) to replace earlier laws aimed at protecting individuals' data. The GDPR places obligations on organizations that collect personal data about EU citizens. Organizations must warn people that their data will be collected. The act also gives people a "right to erasure," meaning they can request to have their personal data erased from a provider's records if the provider has broken any rules or if the individual feels his or her rights have been breached.

THE UNITED STATES

The situation in the United States is different. The right to privacy is not spelled out in the U.S. Constitution, but experts argue that it is implied in laws such as those based on protecting people from an intrusion into their private lives.

WHAT DO YOU THINK?

Who has the right to identify people on social media? Clearly a person has the right to tag him or herself in a photograph, for example. But should someone else be able to tag them without their permission? This could lead to problems if, for example, a person wanted to keep his or her whereabouts hidden, which might be for entirely innocent reasons.

Tag your friend

LEAKED!

In the months before the U.S. presidential election of 2016, thousands of emails were hacked from the account of John Podesta. He ran the election campaign of Hillary Clinton (above, with Barack Obama). The emails were leaked on to the Internet and received lots of media coverage. Many blamed Russia for the cyber attacks, although the Russians denied this. After Donald Trump won the election, he also denied Russian involvement. However, Congress and the FBI both launched investigations into Russian involvement.

TOP SECRET

Other parts of the Constitution that help protect privacy are those that prevent public disclosure of private details, the unauthorized use of individuals' names or photographs, or the creation of false stories about them. However, some experts argue that the lack of an explicit right to privacy means that U.S. courts should impose few restrictions on data collection and its use.

INTERNET SERVICE PROVIDERS

Internet privacy falls under the authority of the Federal Communications Commission (FCC). During the administration of President Barack Obama, the FCC introduced tighter privacy laws. Internet Service Providers (ISPs) were required to gain explicit consent from their customers in order to sell personal information such as their browsing histories. However, in 2017, under president Donald Trump, the Senate narrowly voted to undo these regulations. ISPs claimed that the laws limited their rights under the First Amendment, which guarantees free speech. Their opponents objected that the ISPs merely wanted to make a profit from selling the information. The debate about the changing nature of privacy in the digital world will likely continue for some time into the future.

>> **Google HQ** Should giant Internet companies have an obligation to protect people's privacy?

GLOSSARY

anarchists People who reject any form of authority or established order.

anonymized Data that has had information removed so it cannot be linked to an individual.

antisocial Breaking rules of normal behavior in ways that cause annoyance to others.

barter Exchange goods or services for other goods or services.

biometric Relating to the statistical measurement of biological features.

blackmailers People who demand money in return for not revealing damaging information.

burglary Illegal entry to a building, usually for the purpose of committing a theft.

cache A temporary store on a computer where data is kept to shorten online access times.

civil liberties People's right to be subject only to laws that are established for the good of society.

closed-circuit TV A TV system in which signals are not publicly broadcast but monitored for a particular purpose.

convenience Making it easier to achieve something easily.

database A collection of data stored in a computer in ways that can be easily accessed in various sequences.

data breaches Incidents in which confidential or sensitive information is stolen or viewed by unauthorized users.

data mining Extracting useful patterns from large collections of information stored on a database.

DNA Short for deoxyribonucleic acid, the material by which genetic information is carried from parents to their offspring. DNA is unique to each person, so it is used as a way to identify individuals.

eavesdropped Secretly listened to a private conversation.

hack Access a computer system without authorization.

ISPs Short for Internet Service Providers, companies that provide access to the Internet and services such as website building and data storage.

jurisdictions Geographical regions such as countries in which particular bodies have the right to make laws.

location services Features on cell phones and portable computers that detect the device's geographical location in order to tailor suggestions for the user.

loyalty programs Marketing programs that encourage customers to frequently buy goods or services in return for incentives such as discounts.

statistical Able to be recorded in numerical data.

surveillance The careful watching of a place or an individual, such as a suspected criminal.

FURTHER RESOURCES

Books

Eboch, M M. *Big Data and Privacy Rights*. Essential Library of the Information Age. Minneapolis, MN: Essential Library, 2017.

Harmon, Daniel E. *21st-Century Surveillance Technologies*. Spying, Surveillance, and Privacy in the 21st Century. New York, NY: Cavendish Square Publishing, 2018.

January, Brendan. *Information Insecurity: Privacy Under Siege*. Minneapolis, MN: Twenty-First Century Books, 2016.

Small, Cathleen. *Surveillance and Your Right to Privacy.* Spying, Surveillance, and Privacy in the 21st Century. New York, NY: Cavendish Square Publishing, 2018.

Wilkinson, Colin. *Everything You Need to Know About Digital Privacy.* The Need to Know Library. New York: Rosen Publishing, 2018.

Websites

Data Mining
encyclopedia.kids.net.au/page/da/Data_mining
This page describes data mining and its uses.

How Hackers Work
computer.howstuffworks.com/hacker.htm
How Stuff Works explains how computer hackers operate.

How Security Cameras Work
electronics.howstuffworks.com/gadgets/home/security-cameras.htm
This article from How Stuff Works explains how surveillance cameras work and how they are used.

INDEX